Anything's Poshable

How to adjust your head for the crown

Precious Stevens

Print ISBN: 9798986278810

Library of Congress Control Number:

2022909702

 I have tried to recreate events, locales, and conversations from my memories of them. In order to maintain their anonymity in some instances, I have changed the names of individuals and places, I may have changed some identifying characteristics and details such as physical properties, occupations, and places of residence. This book was self-published by the author with the help of BusyB Writing.

*"I give not because I am rich,
but because I know what it's
like to have nothing."*

--Precious

To my Tribe, without whom this book would have never been written. It was you who helped me find my voice and chase my dreams unapologetically! I write my story in hopes to help you find yours.

CONTENTS.

Anything's Posh-able

INTRODUCTION

I just want to start by saying thank you. It means a lot to me that you took the time to get my book and catch a glimpse into my journey into becoming the woman that I am today. This book serves a few different purposes. For one, it's meant to show you my framework for how you can turn your passion into profit. Believe me when I say that it has NOT been all sunsets and daisies. The process might have seemed like it was quick from the outside looking in, but nobody knew what was going on behind the scenes. There were some blood, sweat, and tears that went into getting this thang going to be the well-oiled machine it is now.

The second thing is when you read my story, I want you to get inspired. I want you to fall back in love with what it is that you truly love to do and allow it to fully blossom to its fullest potential. I want you to complete each chapter's worksheet and begin to visualize your life and how different it could be if you apply some of the action items I discuss in this book. You should *not* be second-guessing yourself at any point in your journey. Now, I know that's easier said than done, but trust me...it can happen. I feel a sense of empowerment every day, waking up to the fact that I built my company from the ground up. Even though it looks easy, it hasn't always been this way.

Believe it or not, I failed at one point. Oh, are you surprised? Yeah, I failed, and I'm not afraid to admit it because you know what? Failure is part of the process. That's just entrepreneurship for you, boo. This journey is going to take you through a bunch of ups and downs, and some of the downs are really, *really* down. However, just because you fall doesn't mean the failure has to be your end result.

So, who should read this? The short answer: entrepreneurs. More specifically, entrepreneurs who are still trying to make sense out of their journey and where they want to go in their careers. Does this sound like you? You may be doing *okay* in your business, but you want *more*. You keep hitting wall after wall as you're trying to grow, but *something* just won't let you be great. You know you can *probably* do the d*mn thing, but you just haven't been put in front of the right resources or people to scale the way you want to. Am I hitting a few nails yet?

I've been there before. A few years ago, I was in your exact same shoes. I knew I wanted more, but I didn't know what more looked like or even how to *get* the "more" that I craved. I wanted to achieve a high level of success, but I didn't have a clue how to go about making it happen. All I had was a breath and a dream. Come to find out, that's all it took. We'll get more into that a little later.

Honestly, this book is for entrepreneurs who need a little extra motivation to keep going. Those who need resources and social proof from a *real* person that it is possible to make 6 and 7 figures doing something they truly love. You don't have to be a celebrity or even have rich parents to make it happen. All you need is the right mindset and the exact blueprint. Luckily, I got the *exact* steps you need to take to see an immediate change within your business. Not in a year or two, but right now.

I wrote this for the people who feel like they will never be able to leave their regular job. Oh yeah...that's a big one. The reason why is because these people feel like they always have to go to work. They feel like they're too old or too comfortable where they are to really go all out for that side hustle that they enjoy so much. Mhm...I'm talking to you too. You need to read this book so you can finally get out of your own head and into this bag.

I want for you to live a more purposeful life. Everything you do from this point on has to have meaning to it. You hear me, sis? I want for you to be intentional about everything, including how you read this book. Think of it like this. How are you going to live a life of purpose if you're out here living so scared that you won't even *attempt* to fulfill your deepest desires? I'll answer that for you, boo. You can't. You won't. But you *will*, and you *can*.

Everything that has ever happened to me has served a purpose; I just didn't see it then. If we're being honest, I thought that I was going through way too much

B.S. to possibly even be on the right track. The longer I stuck with it, the more I started to see what my own purpose was. I am a vessel put on this rock to help people. No matter what capacity, if I'm helping people, then I'm fulfilled and happy.

Since I started my entrepreneurial journey, I've helped thousands of people become better within the premium draping industry. For those of you who aren't familiar with the term or even knew it existed, draping designers are those who create elegant draping, canopies, and backdrops at weddings, baby showers, and other elaborate events. We hold one of the key elements to add the va-va-voom to any event if executed correctly. Just peek at @theposhacademy page on Instagram, Youtube, or Facebook to get a better understanding of just what it looks like.

Between my private Facebook group, YouTube channel, and people who have purchased my courses, I've been able to touch about 52,000 people. No, that is not an exaggeration. We just received our badge for 1 million views on Youtube which indicates that my formula works. In less than 5 years, I've helped 52,000 people get closer to their goal of being a mogul in the draping industry. By sharing my story, I can only pray that I'm able to help twice as many—regardless of what career path they choose.

As you're going through this book, I want to remind you to keep an open mindset. I'm not going to tell you anything too outlandish, but I will be dropping some gems on you that you can use to better yourself and grow your business to where you want it to be. This right here...it's going to be an emotional roller coaster. You'll probably be able to relate to a lot of things that I'm going to share with you, and that's okay. I want you to feel something. I want for you to get so fired up that you're ready to change.

Without any further ado, grab a pen and a cup of tea, and let me show you how to become a boss.

EXERCISE: YOUR CURRENT SITUATION

Before getting started, I want you to think about what made you pick up this book. What do you hope to get out of reading my book? Write your answer below:

I picked up this book because:

____

____

In reading this book, I hope to:

____

____

Right now, I struggle with:

____

____

I am striving to achieve:

____

____

If I have more_________________________, I could really____

____

HUMBLE BEGINNINGS

Once upon a time not long ago... I grew up in the two rival project communities of Cherry Hill and Lexington Terrace in Baltimore, Maryland. It was rough in them streets, and let's just say that life...wasn't that great. My parents suffered from drug addiction, so from the jump, I had a hard time being in any kind of healthy relationship.

My childhood was just as rough as the streets I was living in, and I didn't trust other people the way I probably could have. I won't say I had a chip on my shoulder, but I'll just say that your girl had a hard exterior. When you're trying to survive out there in the projects, you can't show a lot of vulnerability. You have to be tough. Otherwise, people might walk all over you, right?

I kept that same mentality throughout school and into my adult life. Many of the romantic relationships I had were...lackluster to say the least. With all the emotional abuse and turmoil, I believed that this was as good as it was gonna get. The saddest part is that I hadn't realized until much later in life that I was in fact abused. More about that later because they were all just very basic. If you know anything about Precious Stevens, you know there is *nothing* basic about me, okay? So, you can imagine how being in a bland, stagnant relationship could be a real problem for me.

Fast forward to when I met my oldest child's father. We were young in our early 20s trying to be grown. Unfortunately, at that age, life isn't quite figured out. However, I had my own apartment, car, and a good job at The World Trade Center in Baltimore. Things were much tougher for him, and it seemed that he couldn't catch a break. Despite the circumstance, I didn't mind it because he was at least *trying* to do better. We got pregnant in 2000 and things changed drastically; basic was not good enough anymore. Having my son was scary, and I no longer wanted to just *act* like a grown-up. I wanted to *be* a grown-up. I desired for his life to be the total opposite of what mine was. This required me to change the reckless behavior I was accustomed to. In turn, I began to crave a different lifestyle.

Needless to say, we had different agendas which led me to leave when my son was just two years old. Life this way just wasn't good enough anymore. Unfortunately, my son would lose his dad at the tender age of seven to a senseless murder on the rough streets of Baltimore City, just when things were getting great for his dad.

Unfortunate circumstances such as these fed my drive as a hustler. I've always had that, "I'm going to get this money," attitude. With all the bad relationships I've had, the breakup almost always had to do with money. They either weren't making enough money, didn't know how to manage it, or tried to control me with it. Even wayyyy before I started getting into my bag, I knew how to make and manage money.

As soon as I saw that they didn't know how to move with their finances, I was like uh no. I had to exit stage left. My goal is not to bad-mouth any of my past relationships or failed marriages because they taught me so much and prepared me for what was to come. The bottom line is that we had different mindsets, and we were on two separate pages. It just wasn't going to work out the way I wanted it to, so I had to dip.

After my youngest children's father and I split, I was on my own for the first time in God knows how long. I was a newly single mom, and I was all the way independent. I immediately got rid of my pearl white Escalade for a brown minivan. I moved to a different county in a three-story townhouse, and I found a full-time job at HOPE Inc. as a Program Coordinator. It was a non-profit day center for individuals who suffered from homelessness, addiction, or mental health.

The job itself was actually a pretty good gig (or at least at the time). I had my own office with a huge floor-to-ceiling window, was allowed to work remotely, and got along great with the people there. I was responsible for overseeing office operations for the program as well as coordinating the activities for all the members. I planned all the fun stuff like skating, bowling, beach cookouts, fun day in the community, and so much more. This allowed our members to act like children again and have a different experience for those eight hours other than what life was throwing at them out in the rough streets of Baltimore.

Honestly, I can say I was comfortable. I got comfortable because I knew I could take care of my children. I had the freedom to do anything I needed to do to make sure they were good. If something went wrong with my children, they could come to work with me, or I could leave to deal with the school. HOPE pacified me, so I stayed. Not to mention I had the coolest Director ever. Anything I needed within means, the job provided. I was also working part-time as a bartender, and I was able to save all of my income from there because my full-time job paid the bills.

It sounds good on paper, but the reality was that I became stagnant. During the years I was at HOPE, I started to get depressed. I was in such bad shape, sis. The days I was supposed to be at work at 8, I would get there at 11 because I would lay in the bed until 10. Once I finally made it to work, I pushed through from 11 to 2.

While I was there, I can honestly say I really felt like I was needed. I felt like I was serving people, but it still was just something missing. Once it was time to leave, I'd get back into my somber moment. I would come home, prepare dinner, then go back to bed. Once the kids came home, I'd take them to practice, come back home for dinner and a little conversation, then I go back to bed after having my evening cocktail.

Yes, back then I needed that cocktail in order for me to sleep. Don't judge me.

For seven long years, I worked in that position. I had nothing to look forward to, and it was the same ol' thing. I got bored, sis! At the end of the day, it was an ordinary job where I was completely unfulfilled, yet I was okay in a monetary sense. I had a regular life of going to work, going home, taking care of the kids, and going to bed. The same ol' routine of lather, rinse, and repeat.

The one good thing that came from all this was the fact that I was able to save a whole lot of money. Remember, I was a part-time bartender, so I was able to tuck a good $60,000 into the walls of my townhouse. Girl, I told you I was bomb at managing money! Anyway, I just kept stacking and stacking and putting it in the wall. I did that for approximately seven years. I had no inspiration because I was doing that same daily thing. I really thought *that* was what I was supposed to do—work at a regular job and focus on being a mom. It wasn't fulfilling, and I just *knew* I had a bigger purpose. I knew that there was something greater. It just hadn't been introduced to me yet. Was I even prepared if it was? I don't know, all I know is that during that time, I was just existing. I wasn't really living. I was simply waiting...waiting for something to give me purpose outside of being a bomb mother for my kids.

In the meantime, I was going to get myself ready. I figured if something happened, or if I got inspired, or my moment came, I needed to be prepared. I remember saying to myself, *My time is going to come. It just hasn't come yet*. I was just waiting for my ah-ha moment.

***

I ended up dating someone who played a huge role in me finally starting my business. We'll call him Dixon. Dixon and I were old friends from back in the day. He had a crush on me when my oldest son was a kid about 20 years ago. We bumped back into each other because my middle son had a wrestling match out of town that I needed to drop him off at. Being in Mommy-mode, I was kind of a nervous wreck. I couldn't go because I had to work, and I needed someone I trusted to be responsible for my son. I didn't recognize anybody who was going other than the coach, and I was in a frenzy because I was nervous even though all the other kids were without parents too.

While we were walking to the bus, I see Dixon. Mind you, it had been about 15 years since I had last seen him, but I recognized his face immediately. I caught his attention and was like, "Hey, I know I haven't seen you in forever, but I need you to look after my son while y'all on your way to Virginia." Of course, he agreed because he had looked after my oldest son when he was younger as well. We exchanged numbers, and he kept me posted the whole time that they were gone. The bus with the kids didn't come back until later that night, but Dixon made me feel okay with everything the whole time. He dropped my son off, and it was all good.

We talked on the phone the next day, just catching up on everything. He said he wanted to see my oldest, so he met me at my son's football game. Within a few days or so, he secretly moved in. I know I know, what was I thinking right? Well, I wasn't. We already knew each other, so we easily transitioned to being together.

Everything was good until... I got some news. Girl, tell me why I found out that he was married? You know your girl wasn't having that. I told him straight up that I couldn't date a married man, no matter what the circumstance. We ended up breaking up for about a week, then he filed for divorce to prove that he and his wife really were split up.

It worked, lol. So now, we were together-together as one big happy family. Later that year, he invited me to be his date for his sister's wedding. I couldn't remember the last time I attended a wedding, so I happily accepted his invitation. Little did I know, that wedding was going to change more lives than just the bride's...

EXERCISE: YOUR HUMBLE BEGINNINGS

1. What did you want to be when you grew up?

____

____

____

____

2. If you could go back and do it again, would you choose the same dream?

____

____

____

____

3. What advice would you give to someone who is still in school and trying to figure out what they want to be when they grow up?

4. What was the hardest thing about becoming a business owner?

5. What do you love most about being a business owner?

INTEREST PIQUED: THE BIG WEDDING DAY

The days leading up to the wedding were super busy. Everybody in the family, including my boyfriend, helped to put the wedding together. I didn't get to see the actual execution of the setup, but I did know that they worked hard putting everything together the night before. I can't even lie, y'all. I thought that the wedding was going to be basic.

Just the thought of it being put together by the family, I didn't have high hopes. I've never seen a bunch of people be able to put together a whole wedding like that, so my expectations were very low.

It's the wedding day, and we get there early since my

boyfriend was a part of the wedding party. As soon as we got inside the venue, my jaw dropped. It was one of the most beautiful things I had ever seen. Her colors were chocolate and fuchsia, and she had the wedding and reception areas allll the way decked out. It was simply beautiful. They had carving stations, treat tables, decorative centerpieces, coordinated linen, you name it. You know what? Let me go into detail about these decorations because when I tell you my mind was blown!

So, the wedding was the first time I'd ever seen a treat table. There were glass jars filled with different kinds of candies that were the color theme for the wedding. There were little fuchsia and chocolate accents scattered throughout the venue..The linen was a chocolate color, and even the napkins had small intricate details. Everything was so meticulously put together with not even a fork out of place. It truly looked like a page straight out of a magazine.

What had me was the fact that no professionals did this. They didn't pay any big design companies to come in and make it look like that. This was all done by regular people who came together for a common goal. The whole time I admired not only the decorations but also the *effort* that went into it. The newlyweds, the guests, and everybody in between were having an amazing time. At that moment, I saw creativity tie into putting people into a joyous and fun moment. A spark started to ignite within me, and I finally felt something. Something I hadn't felt in a long time—excitement.

On the way home from the wedding, I couldn't stop talking about how pretty everything looked. I was so hyped about what I saw, and I just knew that I could do something like that too. We had a nice 90-minute drive to get home, so he got an earful of everything I was feeling.

"You all really did a phenomenal job," I gushed as I thought about all the fine details that were put into the decorations.

"Thanks, I think it turned out nice," he agreed.

"You know, I can really do something like that."

"Oh, really? You want to do wedding decorations?"

"Yeah...yeah, I really do."

"Alright, let's do it."

"I am. I think I can do this."

"Well, you just let me know when you ready. Whatever you want to do, we'll do it."

Pause. Let me just say this about the man I was with at this time. He was very supportive of any and everything that I wanted to do. I could say I wanted to fly a dang purple kite, and he'd say, "Okay, cool." That's just how he was.

I know in the back of his mind he was wondering if I was serious. Truthfully, I am that type to come up with an idea and just leave it. But this here? This sparked something in me. That night when I went to sleep, my mind was racing with all the possibilities of where this new world could take me. I was a little intoxicated from enjoying the festivities, but my mind was made up. I had to see if I could take this somewhere.

EXERCISE: YOUR INTEREST PIQUED

1. How did you first get interested in business?

____

____

____

____

2. What inspired you to become your own boss?

____

____

____

____

3. How have you been able to maintain your creative spark while also being a business owner?

____

____

____

4. What do you think is the biggest challenge that creative entrepreneurs face when it comes to running their own businesses?

____

____

____

5. What advice would you give to someone who is thinking about starting their own business?

____

____

____

GET INTO IT

When I wake up the next day, I'm fired up. I'm super excited and still thinking about everything I saw the night before at the wedding. Now, me being me, if I remember correctly, I *know* I called out. My job was super supportive, and I could literally say the most random thing and it was never an issue.

Well, a few times I was reprimanded for abusing my privileges, but I'm sure that was to appease my co-workers. I would wake up and say, "Boss, I only got three tires on my car. I can't make it to work." And guess what? It *always* flew. It doesn't matter what crazy requests or reasons I came up with, they were going to be okay with whatever I said. So, I used that to my advantage.

After coming up with some random reason to not

come in, I had to call my bestie to let her know where my mind was. There aren't too many decisions that I can make without getting her input. I'd be lying to y'all if I said I remembered the exact conversation, but it went a little something like this:

"Yoyo!"

"Hey, Peach! What's up?"

"Girl, you know how I went to that wedding yesterday?"

"Yeah, how was it?"

"Girlllllll...let me tell you something. I did not know what to expect, but I wasn't expecting *that*!"

"Oh, Lord? Was it bad?"

"Girl, no, it was the opposite. I saw the most beautiful setup I've ever laid eyes on, and to think that the family put all that together in what? A day?"

"Forreal? What did everything look like?"

"Like something out of a magazine, yo. Long story short, I want to do it."

She paused for a second. "You mean like do it, do it? Setting up weddings and stuff?"

"Yes! Why not?"

"Shoooooot you know I'm here for it. You been so out of it lately, and I want you to really dive into this to get that spark back into your life that you've been missing. So, what do we need to do first?"

Just like that, I had my bestie's blessing, and we started brainstorming ideas on how I could make this happen. I ended up making a Zoom call and getting my squad on board as well. These chicks are my day 1's and have supported my ventures since doing hair at 12 years old. After consulting with them and my boyfriend, we came up with a pink-themed color scheme because I just had to have me some pink in there somewhere. It was one of my favorite brand colors at the time, so pink had to be part of it.

Once we got the colors, we needed to come up with a business name. About four different ideas got thrown around, like Precious Creations, but I just wasn't feeling it. I didn't want to go with something generic that had my name in it for a couple of reasons. For one, with my name being Precious, I didn't want for clients to be turned off and assume I was hood.

Secondly, I had a vision for where I wanted it to go and reusing a business name that I had when I was making jewelry just wasn't going to cut it. I wanted something bigger and bolder than that. So, I started thinking more about my attitude and what I wanted to deliver when it came to my services. I Googled different words to describe something that was elegant and luxurious, and then I came across the word posh. Posh was equivalent to exquisite (which was heavily used in the design space), plus it started with a P like my name. I knew I had to have posh incorporated into my brand some kind of way, so I kept brainstorming. At the time, I only wanted to focus on design, so I added the word design to the mix and Posh Designs was born!

From there, I got back on Google and learned about Periscope, Fiverr, and all those freelancing sites, and I found someone to make me a $5 logo that same day. Y'all, I was not playing any games. I sent different design ideas to my girls, and they were all very supportive of where I was trying to go with this new business endeavor.

To be honest, this whole point in time felt like a big blur because it happened so fast. I went to that wedding on a Tuesday and by Friday I had a full business. Everything changed for me at that point. I was so excited to be doing something new and different that I had hit the ground running. Shoot, I even found myself going to work a little earlier just so I could work on my business. Even though I was super pumped up, I was focusing on all the wrong things. We'll talk more about that in the next chapter. For now, let me finish telling you about how much this new business venture consumed me.

***

It really felt like a rebirth. My bestie Yo-yo went to file my business license at the state office building that Friday. I went shopping for all the things that I thought I needed to recreate what I saw at that wedding. I was getting balloons, treats, treat table decor, and everything else you can think of.

Remember, I had a couple of coins saved up in my wall safe, so it wasn't a problem to spend it to get my supplies. I told myself that I'd allow myself to use $5,000 of that reserved cash to invest in this new business.

Little did I know I would end up spending triple that amount. I had a 1,800-square-foot townhouse at the time, so I was able to stash all the new goodies all over the place. I was couponing, so one side was for my couponing stuff and the other side was for Posh Designs. Eventually, I bought so much stuff that my house was overflowing with event design supplies. It even got to the point to where I had to kitty-corner my sofa, so I could put more materials behind it. Yes, it was that serious!

I still remember my kids' reactions when they saw me putting pipe kits and treat table supplies under the bed. On one hand, they were interested and excited because they got to taste the treats and help me tap into my creative side even more. On the other side, they weren't thrilled about having to help me set up at different events. To this day, they always mention how proud they were of me stepping out and doing something different like that. It even inspired them to get into their own business mindsets once they got older.

As for work, they didn't even realize how distracted I was. I'm the type who loves to have things done early and in advance, so I don't have to worry about it. I can't stand waiting until the last minute to get something done because my anxiety starts to kick in. So, all my work responsibilities were scheduled and prepared several months out. When I was at the office, I was really just there for show because my work had already been completed. Each day I was at work, I was working vigorously on Posh Designs, LLC.

After I got all my supplies and a little more knowledge of the industry, I started to learn more about social media and what it had to offer. I got on Pinterest and started creating different boards to help give me inspiration for new designs. I got on Instagram, stopped following actual people, and searched for event decor companies instead.

I would also go to pages that promoted other businesses that use their products to help me find even more information about supplies, décor ideas, etc. I would soak up all that information for hours at a time and buy my stuff the next day.

A whole new world opened up to me because prior to that, I was just playing with social media. I was on there posting my little butt pics and doing all the crazy stuff we do when we don't have anything else going on. Now, it's a whole 360. I found myself cleaning up my pages and joining these groups that I've never even heard of. I really had no clue that people were doing event design to that magnitude.

I kept asking for help and trying to go to these different groups to gain resources on how to do everything, but no one was reaching out. I may have contacted over 100 different people, and not many were forthcoming with providing the information I needed to be successful. On top of that, the information I was given was the bare minimum. I couldn't believe it.

There's no question that the struggles I endured when I first started were the catalysts that made me create The Posh Academy. I'll go deeper into that later, but just know that when I say no one was trying to give any support or answers, I do mean NOBODY.

In hindsight, I was just going for it. I didn't have a clue what to do; all I knew was that everything needed to be pretty. Life was pretty much smooth sailing for the first few months. I was happy, I was getting steady clients, and I was able to still fulfill my regular job duties at the nonprofit. I say that to say this: people that have a 9-5 that want to transition to full-time entrepreneurship, don't quit in the beginning. I actually had my job for two years before I quit. Having a full-time job while pursuing your passion is a lot, but it's worth it to have that cushion just in case things don't take off the way you want them to.

So, the first year was just me learning at work and building my thought wallet. Even if I was at a game or something with the kids, I was on my phone or the computer looking at treat tables and learning how to buy stuff. Honestly, I didn't even realize how the neglect started. I started neglecting responsibilities, children, work, and everything else because I was fully immersed in this new business. I didn't know it, but I was about to wake up from my dream and find myself in a full-fledged nightmare.

EXERCISE: HOW DID YOU GET INTO IT?

1. What made you decide to become a creative?

____

____

____

____

2. Do you remember what your first creative project was?

____

____

____

____

3. How did your family and friends react when you told them you wanted to be a creative?

____

____

____

4. What was the hardest thing about becoming a business owner?

____

____

____

YEAR 1: THE NIGHTMARE

As I'm living my best life and buying up centerpieces, linen, and everything else that I can think of that deals with décor, I also started to get a few events booked up by friends and family. I used those events to get my name put out there and get as many pictures as possible to push Posh Designs.

For the first few months, it was a bartering situation. They would buy the supplies, and I would do the designs and get photo-ops for my portfolio. I didn't mind doing it because I wanted to attract the right kind of clients anyway.

I still remember my very first home event. It was the

first time I would get to do a treat table for a holiday party that my best friend was giving that year. She normally didn't have a treat table set up at their holiday soiree, but being my bestie, she wanted to support my new business venture. So, I made her a treat table that was the focal point of the whole set-up. The guests loved it, even though it had a lot of flaws. I had paint cans holding up certain display parts, a plastic Christmas-themed tablecloth that acted as a backdrop taped to the wall, and treats that looked like a kindergartener made them.

Looking back, it was really unprofessional. I could have done so much better, and I remember feeling disappointed in myself because I wasn't able to execute it the way I envisioned it. I wanted to recreate what I saw at that wedding, and this treat table just wasn't giving me life like I wanted it to.

After that, each event I did was just me winging it and trying to go off of memory. I would try to remember how I saw the different levels on the tables and this and that, but I fell short. All the Pinterest pins and Youtube tutorials available at the time were subpar and just weren't giving me the resources I needed. I still had paint cans here and there, hiding the evidence with flowers or something cute that went with the décor. People seemed to really enjoy what I was doing, but I didn't. I completely felt like I was coming up short.

I kept on researching and watching people do different designs and set-ups. I swear I was looking for hours, but I wasn't very successful with execution. E6000 glue had become my best friend, and I felt like I was becoming the DIY queen. Again, everybody *liked* what I was doing, but I didn't have any of my professional tools yet. As a result, I wasn't producing that wow factor that I was looking to have that would live up to the Posh name.

All my children's birthdays were within 3 months of each other. I ended up decorating their birthdays using flimsy backdrops, PVC pipe canopies, and other DIYs that I found on the internet. With that canopy in particular for my son's 16th birthday party, I was scared out of my mind. I swear to God, y'all, I was terrified that the thing was going to collapse while the teenagers were dancing all over the place.

Thankfully it didn't, but those experiences had me on edge. I was an actual company, so I would be liable for *anything* that happened. If something was to break or hurt somebody, I knew I could be sued or get into trouble. With that in mind, I was determined to get everything set up the professional way. I kept telling myself I was better than this. I had more to offer than the work that I was producing.

I even remember putting together one of my cousin's Dallas Cowboy-themed baby showers. Just like with the other events, I just couldn't figure out how to make this draping thing work. I got pieces of fabric and tried to swoop them here and there, but I just didn't feel comfortable. I didn't know what I was doing. I see photos now, and I'm like, "What the hell was I doing?" It really was all I knew at the time, and it showed.

After the first few months, I started trying to find actual clients instead of bartering services. I came up with different strategies to attract people, and for a while, it seemed like it worked. I was booked every weekend, and I felt like I was super busy and making it. When I was working at my 9-5, I may have been making around $30,000 a year. My weekly paychecks were in the $500 range. Now, I was making that by doing just one party. Ya girl felt like she was on top of the world.

Then...reality set in.

I felt like I was really doing something big because I didn't know about the *business* side of running a business. I was so focused on making everything look good and getting supplies that I didn't stop to think about the return on my investment. When I say investment, I'm not just talking about money but the time I was putting in as well. During that second half of the year, I was so frustrated. I refused to tap into any more of my hard-earned cash to buy cuter inventory. I was tired of shopping for inventory, coming home tired, exhausted, and overworked to the point I felt unmotivated. I wasn't feeling fulfilled in my end results. I got tired of the $500, $800, and $1,000 parties. I *knew* this couldn't be it. I could tell that I was growing mentally, but I still wasn't feeling like all I put into the business was worth it.

Basically, I was looking for a higher clientele. I *knew* what I wanted to do, but I didn't know *how* to go about it. I didn't know what the problem was. Why weren't these high rollers attracted to my business? What was I doing wrong? At this point, I just wanted to give up. I said to myself, "Nah, I'm just going to stay comfortable because at least I know I'm getting a paycheck every week." Trying to go out here and find somebody to book this event then I got to *work* the event... it just wasn't what I wanted. Mentally, I was drained and felt like I was wasting my time.

What really became the turning point that gave me that "aha!" moment was when I started my road to personal development. I thought that since I had a logo, colors, and (don't laugh) someone else's mission statement, I was in a good position to get some coaching to take myself to the next level. My coach at the time gave me some homework to work on, and I couldn't do it to save my soul! It was all foundational stuff, but I struggled to get through all the worksheets because I had not properly built my foundation. Y'all, I was up 'til 3 and 4 in the morning crying because I was so frustrated. I thought that there was *no* way that this should be that hard.

I was so upset that I was ready to fire my coach. Little did I know, *she* was ready to fire *me*. If someone asked me about my business and why I did what I did, I couldn't answer them. To say the least, it was embarrassing that I had no idea of my why, let alone what made me stand out enough to hire me over my competition. That was the pivotal moment that made me realize I had to do something. I was gonna keep hitting brick wall after brick wall if I didn't completely revamp what I had tried to build.

I had a choice I needed to make. I could just stop cold turkey and go back to work, or I could give this thing one last go-'round and put my true all into it. I'm not a quitter, so I decided to give it another shot. I invested heavily in becoming certified, building my foundation, and really focusing on my why so that I could better position Posh Designs.

EXERCISE: YOUR YEAR 1 EXPERIENCE

1. Everyone has struggles with their business at some point, what was the worst moment for you?

____

____

____

____

2. What advice would you give to someone who is just starting out in their creative field?

____

____

____

____

3. What was a time when you didn't think your business wouldn't make it, but it did?

___

4. How do you deal with self-doubt when it comes to your business?

5. Are there any techniques or strategies you used that others could benefit from?

6. What would you say is the biggest lesson you've learned about owning your own business?

STEP BACK: DISCOVERY OF MY WHY

Before we continue with the story, I want to take a moment to really talk to you about my why because it truly helped shape my business and the way I carry myself today. Before I had an epiphany and revamp, I didn't understand the depth of my "why." At first, it was pretty much a cookie-cutter answer if anyone were to ask.

Even today, when I'm coaching and ask people what *their* why is, they give me something generic. I'm sure you've heard it all before. Most of them say, "Well, I want to leave something to my kids," or "I want to be financially free." That's all well and good, but realistically it's *much* deeper than that.

Until I learned and trained myself on the strategies that I now teach others, I was just as lost as them. Now, don't get me wrong. The answers they gave me weren't *wrong;* they just weren't *enough.* You say you want financial freedom? Okay, fine. *Why* do you want financial freedom? It's not enough to say that you want to be debt-free or want to live comfortably. You have to add some meaning to it as well.

For me, it was because I knew what it was like to be broke. I know what it's like to lose a parent and have nothing secured for you. I've seen firsthand what it is to be poor and not have anything. There have been nights when I had to go hungry because there was no food in the fridge. Even worse, we'd steal groceries from the store, y'all! Some days, I had to go to school wearing my cousin's clothes and shoes because mine were raggedy. I've lived in poverty before, so there *was* no other option for me. I had to make this work because I refused to go back to what I used to be.

Funny thing: I'm writing about it now, but it took me a *long* time to even say this stuff out loud. It was hard for me to accept or even *think* about the life I used to have when I was younger. The reason being is because when you're determining your why and understanding that it's not a general question, you start noticing some things.

For me, I discovered that a lot of what I was dealing with in my new business was attached to childhood trauma. I had to relive a lot of the stuff I endured as a kid in order to really gain healing from it. I didn't realize it, but even at 38 years old, I was still being held captive to that damn five-year-old little girl I used to be.

I'll be real with you. So many things that happen in business, meaning a lot of our struggles and frustrations, really stem from inner things that we dealt with in our past. It just attaches itself to certain situations that we go through, whether it's a relationship, your business, parenting style, or something else. It can show up in any kind of way, but when it *does* show up, you have to do the work to get through it. It's not something you can just surpass and push to the back of your mind. If you try to, then I hate to break it to you, but that shit is gonna keep coming up. I would know...because I tried it.

You have to deal with whatever it is head-on. It sounds scary, I know, but it's necessary for your growth as an entrepreneur and as a person. Personally, I dealt with it by just being honest with myself and saying things aloud. It's one thing to say something in your head, but it's something else entirely to admit it out in the open and make it real.

I had to understand that if I didn't deal with it and break free of the grasp it had on my life, I would forever run into frustrations. I had to let go and forgive if I was ever going to be happy. If I didn't, all I would do is continue to take it out on people who don't even deserve it.

Now, we all know how easy it is to say something but not really do it. Yep, I know I'm guilty of that from time to time. Again, I had to be realistic with myself about this forgiveness thing. I had to commit to really going through with it and not just *saying* I would. After all, I wouldn't be fooling anyone but myself if I tried to do anything otherwise, right? I had to be open and honest about the fact that I held a lot of animosity toward my mother.

We all get like that towards people we trust and care

about. They do what they do, and we hold that against them for years. You can't live like that, boo. You can't hold all that hatred and negativity in your spirit if you want to see success. You have to learn how to just let it go.

Believe me, I know it's hard! Still, you have to think about it from a different perspective. Instead of feeling like they *intentionally* meant to hurt you or do you wrong, try thinking of it like this. "I know this person did whatever they did, but they gave me the best that they had. They showed up in whatever capacity they knew how, and that's all they could do."

See, the problem is that we tend to look for certain people to do things for us or treat us a certain way. We have a lot of expectations, not realizing that these people *can't* give what they don't *have*. And guess what? That is okay! There's no need to feel any kind of way about a past situation. What's done is done, and you have to accept it. *I* had to understand that and be cool with it.

It's a big deal when your biggest disappointments are the relationships you have with the people who created you. My dad passed away when I was 19. I was lost, hurt, and emotionless. My dad was the coolest guy I ever met. Unfortunately, his battle with drug addiction would determine his destiny early. I was angry for a very long time because I felt that he chose that lifestyle over me. I would imagine as a little girl calling my dad once I got older to do anything and everything I needed. He was the most talented person I ever met. He could fix cars, homes, sing or crooning rather, dance, tell jokes and dress his behind off! I knew that whatever I needed, Q-Ball could do it! Well, those dreams ended abruptly right after I graduated and got my first apartment. I mean, who the hell was gonna fix my car if it broke down? I just entered adulthood and had no guidance. I was torn, and I carried that hurt for most of my adulthood.

Now my mom on the other hand, for the longest time, I had not many words for her because nothing I had to say was positive. It took a long time for me to understand that she did what she could, and that was all she had. If her situation was different, I'm almost certain that my outcome would have been different. However, that's a whole other part of being human. People are who they are, and everything happens the way it's supposed to.

I knew that until I could get past what I was feeling, I couldn't be who I was meant to be. I had to just accept and forgive her. And I mean *really* forgive her. That meant that I had to have that conversation with my mother and tell her how I really felt. Truthfully, she probably knew it already because of how I treated her. Still, as part of my healing and self-development, I had to verbalize it to her in order for it to be real. I had to tell her, "I was disappointed in you for a long time, but now, I forgive you." As much as it hurt to say out loud and probably even more for her to hear, it was necessary. It was a breakthrough that really changed my perspective on how I lived, worked, and dealt with other people.

I didn't know it at the time, but as I reflect now, I can say that the strained relationship with my mother along with my rough childhood affected my business in a few different ways. One way is that it motivated me to keep pushing because there was always the fear that I was one decision away from being in the same situation she was. In my mind, I couldn't relax. I couldn't relax then, and I still can't now because I *know* what it looks like on the other side. I've been exposed to what it's like to just survive and not live.

Therefore, I don't have a choice. There are no safeguards for me if I fail; I have to get it while the getting is good. Giving up is not in my vocabulary, okay?!

Another way I was affected was in my ability to trust. To be blunt, I was terrified. I never fully trusted the men I was with. I also was super terrified because in this business—and honestly in any business—one of the things you have to do constantly is network and join collaborations and partnerships.

For me, because I had a damaged relationship with my mom, it was hard for me to trust anybody. A lot of times, something beneficial for me would arise, but my trust factor was so jacked up that I dropped the ball. The littlest thing would come up, and I'd be quick to say, "No, I'm good. I'm cool." You might be looking at this now thinking, "Really, Precious?" but girl, you have to understand. I've had some of my biggest heartbreaks from my parents. As a child, that does something to you. As an adult, it resonates and sticks with you. Think about it, if I couldn't even trust my parents, how was I supposed to trust someone I didn't even know? I'll tell you how: I couldn't!

That fear of broken trust kept me to myself and prevented me from connecting with other people. Something I experienced in my childhood completely stunted my growth as an entrepreneur. I couldn't grow the way I should have because I didn't trust anyone, and I was scared to let someone else in because I *knew* they would disappoint me. I had low expectations of everyone, y'all!

This spilled over in my romantic life too which is why I was settling for the basics. I felt that the people (my parents) who were supposed to have loved me most and protect me dropped the ball so everyone else would surely do the same. If it weren't for me taking that step back and discovering my why, then I might have never been able to uncover that trauma. I may have never been able to completely forgive my parents and allow myself to grow and build solid relationships with others.

I say all that for this takeaway: look deeply and reflect on your why *before* you dive into other aspects of getting your business together. You may uncover some things that you need to deal with mentally before starting to flourish.

EXERCISE: YOUR WHY

1. Why did you decide to become an entrepreneur?

   ____

   ____

   ____

2. How do you stay motivated when things get tough?

   ____

   ____

   ____

3. What would your life look like when your business achieves the level of success you desire?

   ____

   ____

   ____

4. Who will your success be able to impact?

____

____

____

5. How will you impact these people?

____

____

____

6. What does success mean to you?

____

____

____

COMPLETE REVAMP

I don't remember the *exact* timeframe it took me to figure everything out. However, I know that I did a lot of deep diving to understand who I was and, most importantly, who I wanted to be. I had to ask myself a lot of questions that, at the time, I wasn't ready to answer. As a result, I started to learn more about the business side of entrepreneurship and understand different things that I had ignored initially.

For instance, I found out how to identify more with my audience, find my avatar, and even create my own messaging. When I first started my business, I really just went with whatever sounded good. I would see someone else's story and be like, "Oh, her message sounds cute. Let me use that!" There was no reason or strategy behind how I was communicating with my audience or even how I went about creating my messaging. *That's* why my business wasn't flourishing the way I thought it should have. I had been doing it wrong for almost a year.

Basically, nothing I did was resonating with me because it did not come from me. It was not my authentic self; it was a mixture of other people's. My brand hadn't come from me setting realistic goals and creating my why. I was so excited to just do something new that I didn't take my time and set a solid foundation.

Once I had this epiphany, I went full throttle to make this thing work out. I got serious about Posh Designs and started to look at it as more than just a business that could make me some side coins. Unfortunately, the more focused I got on the business, the more conflict I caused with my job. There were times that it would take me 10 minutes to realize that someone was trying to get my attention because I was too busy researching something about my business.

Just when things started to take a turn for the better, I found myself conflicted again. On the one hand, I wanted to fulfill my duties at my job because it was a steady paycheck. I knew what to expect, and I knew how to do my job well. Although I wasn't happy, it was very comfortable. On the other, I couldn't help but wonder... if I could get up and work for these people, then why can't I put that same energy into my own business?

Naturally, I had a shift in my mentality. Not only was I working on my business, but I started working on myself on a personal level too. I started reading and listening to more books so that I could be motivated and enlightened. In particular, I want to put you up on game with one called *The Five Second Rule* by Mel Robbins. Y'all...that book did so much for my personal development. Reading that book made me realize just how much of a procrastinator I was. If I don't want to do something, I will keep on putting it off because I just don't want to deal with it. That book taught me how to be more productive, and it made me better understand my thought process in how I work.

On top of that, I learned a lot of things about myself too. Back then, I thought I was really extra. While reading the book, I got introduced to something called the DISC personality test. At first, I thought it was a load of B.S., but then after I actually took the test, things started to make sense. I was finally able to understand *why* I moved the way that I moved. Most importantly,

I realized that I *am* the sh*t; I'm just a little different.

For instance, I ask a lot of questions because I enjoy learning new things. Some people might misinterpret that to mean that I'm hard to get along with or nosey. Shoot, even *I* thought I was just difficult at first. The truth is that I truly just want to know what's going on. I need to fully understand what is happening because, to be candid, you ain't going to just tell me *anything* and expect me to take your word for it. I've never been that kind of person, and I was not about to *become* her either.

Up until this point, I was just going with the flow. I was trying hard to make everything work, but I always had a little bit of imposter syndrome going on. It took me stepping back and understanding myself before I could get comfortable and confident in my abilities. Once that confidence hit, baby, it soared through the *roof*.

Now, certain conversations don't even entertain me. I need to be attached or heavily vested in something to be inspired and empowered. If it can't hold my interest, I'm good just sitting in the corner by myself.

I started to be more intentional on the social media pages I followed and the content I allowed myself to digest. Slowly, I found myself adapting to a new lifestyle. I started adopting automation tools and management systems to make my business run seamlessly. I started getting into more audiobooks when I didn't have time or patience to sit and read a physical one. Even if I was just in the car on the way to the store, I would go ahead and listen to a book. My whole mindset was changing, and I didn't want to have an opportunity for it to get off track.

Another thing I did during this revamp was immediately stopped buying inventory. I just saw all this money going out and nothing coming in. It was stressful, and I knew I had to get my foundation together before spending another penny on supplies. Although I said I'd spend about six months trying to get my business foundation in order, the reality is that it took almost a year. Even though it took longer than I initially anticipated, it was sooo worth it.

Now, I was getting the itch of Posh Designs no longer being a lucrative hobby. I was starting to have thoughts of, "Hey, I could possibly leave my job if I get this right." I knew if I wanted to get deep into it, what

I did in the past wouldn't work. I needed to make a *drastic* change. The change had to happen not just in myself but in how I was dealing with the people I loved as well. I had to have conversations with my family members about what would happen. I was about to go into beast mode and get *really* selfish.

Prior to this, I was a house mom. Practice, dinner, activities—that was my life. Now, I was so engrossed in my business I had to get real with my kids and the rest of my family. Even if I'm at a game, I may be reading. I might be on my phone or researching something on my computer at any given moment. See, they weren't used to *that* kind of mom. Being a business mom was going to be a whole new ball game, and I had to make sacrifices if I wanted to secure the home.

At that time, my daughter was maybe about 9, my middle son was 11, and my oldest son was about 16. I knew they needed me, and I wanted to be there as their mother. At the same time, I had a business to build. I was determined to make it happen, so I made it clear to them what it was about to be like while I was in this transition.

As for the revamp itself, nothing changed aesthetically with my business. I still had the same old website that was barely functioning. I had the same logo and colors. I was starting from ground zero, but with *my* messaging and *my* purpose. I really had to think about what I was doing and who I wanted to serve. So, I started to survey the people I was working with. It's funny because when I was first told to do these things by my coach, I didn't want to do it. I was like, "Yeah ain't nobody got time for all that." But remember, ya girl was determined! Despite my reservations, I did it anyway.

Once I started seeing the results, something happened. I found myself falling in love with just doing the dag-gone work! The process I had for making myself better became my strategy for working with others. I always would go and question the people I was working with. Asking them about their why and their passion and purpose. Doing so helped me really strengthen my business and get a solid core before I went and did any of the physical branding.

Now, when I finally got to the aesthetic/branding stage, I knew exactly what to say. I wasn't just copying off someone else's website. People told me how I helped them and why they came to me. They told me why they liked me, so I knew what to say to attract those same types of people. I was not only positioning my brand and my business to be heavy competition in the marketplace, but I also had to make sure I had what people were looking for. The solutions that I provided needed to be heard and felt deeply in my marketing strategies.

As everything was blossoming in front of my eyes, it felt like a rebirth. Honestly, it felt like a new business. I was eliminating parts of the business that I didn't like. So along with that revamp, I got clearer on what I enjoyed. I fell in love with the core, which was draping. Everything I was doing was shaping my business for growth. I was molding it to be what I wanted it to be.

I was falling in love with my clients because I was getting *better* clients. Why? Because I was talking to the people I *wanted* to talk to. I was learning how my message could attract the people I *wanted* to work it. I was laser-focused on designing and developing a business that ultimately was going to sustain me. I wanted something to help me reach the potential I knew I had.

I always knew I was so much more than the mediocrity I was producing. All I needed was the know-how to put all the elements in place to help me achieve those goals. The only thing that prevented me from success at that point was the stuff I *didn't* know. I already had the work ethic, so all I had to learn was the stuff I didn't know to get the things I didn't have.

***

As an aside, I want to add that I had an amazing support system. Sometimes, my support system believed in me when I didn't believe in my *damn* self. I'd be on the phone during one of my frustrating moments, wanting to give up. They wouldn't allow me.

My kids were some real troopers. They didn't even care if we had to eat dinner in the van. If anything, they pushed me to keep going. They would periodically tell me that they were proud of me and that they would stick beside me throughout my journey. Even if we all had to band together with balloons over our heads in the truck, they were all in.

Honestly, I don't even think I would have had my

business if it wasn't for them. I really don't because they got me through some of the roughest times. I know some people out there have no one like that. They don't have any type of support or cheerleaders to help them through those tough times. If this is the case there are a few options still available such as:

- Find accountability partners
- Find a great mentor or coach
- Surround yourself with like minded individuals
- Take a self assessment test and get more intimate with yourself

Truth is, I can go on and on about how to become your own cheerleader because I had to do all those and more.

Even though I had great support in the beginning, it's wise to be aware that it may not last forever. I thank God that I had a great support system in the beginning because this made it easier for the next phase to take place.

EXERCISE: YOUR BUSINESS REVAMP

1. What are the main things you need to improve in your creative business?

___

___

___

2. How do you feel when it comes to promoting your work?

___

___

___

3. What is the toughest part of running a business?

___

___

___

4. Are there any tools or techniques you'd like to learn more about?

___

___

___

5. How do you maintain work/life balance with your creative business?

___

___

___

6. How do you know when it's time to pivot and change your business model?

___

___

___

7. Why do you think some businesses succeed while others fail?

___

___

___

8. How important is creativity in business?

___

___

___

ON TO BIGGER AND BETTER THINGS

When 2018 hit, I had done all I could do at the job, so I had to quit. It was honestly just weird how it all happened. The company was making some shifts in management and operations. For the past few years, I had been pretty much coasting because I had some of the best incentives the company had to offer. I was working part remote and part in the office, so I didn't really have to worry about a whole lot when it came to flexibility. Well, when the shift in management started, so did the B.S. *Now*, suddenly, upper management didn't like the working arrangements that I had.

They came to me and gave me some alternatives, but I didn't like any of them. In the back of my mind, I wasn't surprised. I *knew* this day was going to come. The day that I would have to make a decision about what my next move was going to be. Was I going to stop my business and continue with my mediocre job or keep investing in it and watch it grow? Well, it was a no-brainer because, at that point, I was well vested in Posh Designs and had just started The Posh Academy. So... I made plans to exit stage-left.

Not only was my job in limbo (*they* didn't know that), but I had other things on my mind as well. Even though Baltimore was my home, I knew that for me to get any kind of great measure of success, I had to leave. I don't know what came over me, but I was like, "You know what? It's time for me to let go of people, places, and things that no longer serve me." Just like that, I started making plans to get out of Baltimore.

At first, I was just playing around, not even thinking it was going to happen. I started filling out applications in states I dreamt of living in. The same way that my business seemed like it happened overnight is how I ended up finding myself a new place to call home.

I had a lot of PTO accumulated at my job, so my plan was to cut and run as I knew I was approved for a new house in Atlanta. I was gonna drive down there, finish my housing process, and not tell anyone I was leaving. For some reason, it didn't feel real to me yet, so I didn't feel like it was time to start saying good-byes or anything.

After I applied for the house, everything went fast. I closed 30 days later, had a whole wedding 2 days after I closed, and prepared myself to make the biggest move of my life. When I say no one knew what all I was doing outside my immediate family and my best friend, I mean *no one*. When I was approved for my house, I had to go back home and have these serious conversations.

I didn't think it would be so easy. My fiancé and I had the conversation about moving before I even really thought about it. I was trying to choose between Atlanta, Florida, and Philly. I only thought about Philly because I would have been closer to home, but the taxes were ridiculous. After I told him my plans, he went and had a couple of conversations with his contractors, and he was fine. Remember, he drove trucks so he pretty much could be wherever he wanted to be. So, he told me I could go wherever I wanted to go.

Next, were the kids. My plan was for all my kids to come down to Atlanta and stay with me, hence why I got a five-bedroom house. There were good and bad reactions when I told them the news. My daughter was super excited because she was pretty much with me throughout the whole process.

Now, my oldest son was already away from home because he had a family. So, he stayed in Baltimore with them. My middle son was kind of torn, and he wasn't too sure what he wanted to do. I thought it would be a great decision because he was just entering as a teenager and was beginning to get into lots of trouble. I certainly wasn't going to *make* him leave, so he stayed back in Baltimore with his dad so they could work on their relationship. This allowed him to continue with his sports team and maintain his friendships.

My best friend didn't realize how serious I was. At first, she thought I was playing. Then, once it really hit her, it was like the life got sucked out of her. I understood her concern, but I was so excited that I just went for it.

As for my job, I wanted and needed them to fire me point-blank. So, I made that happen. Within three weeks, I had signed on a house, got married, quit my job, and moved out of Baltimore, Maryland.

***

When I first came to Atlanta, I had like a little mini nervous breakdown the second day. Think about it. I didn't have a job anymore. I went and bought a house in a new state with *no* job. All I had was a dream and faith. My faith was so big because there was *no* plan B for me. This was it, and I was going to make sure I put myself in the position where my business had to work because I had real responsibilities.

Truth be told, it was scary. Still, I just went full throttle in my business. Even choosing that particular house was a strategy. I knew my house had to have everything I needed to run my business. I knew I needed an office. I knew I needed 18-foot ceilings in order to practice my draping. I wasn't looking for just a house; I was looking for an opportunity. This house was more than just a home. It was my fresh start.

Even though I was happy, I did go through a grieving period. We felt lost. The move put a lot of friction on the family dynamic. I remember one time, my oldest son had a moment where he felt like I just left. My youngest son was talking like he didn't make the right decision. All in all, it really kind of hurt our relationship a little bit. Up until that point, it was always just *us*. Now, it was like we were broken. Even my daughter felt it because she didn't have her brothers. She was 800 miles away from her entire family and being uprooted from that definitely caused some negative feelings. I started to have some thoughts as to whether or not I moved too fast with the move. But you know what? Sometimes, you have to just go with your gut. I knew that I was doing what was best for me long-term, but I just wasn't feeling that way when I first got to Georgia.

As for business, it picked up just where it had left off in Baltimore. By the time I got settled in Atlanta, it had already transitioned to me being less of a worker bee and more of an influencer or teacher/coach. I had a couple of planners and designers reach out to me, and they helped me get started as an instructor. I was even able to have my first draping class because of these young ladies. One of them worked at a hotel, so she was the connection for a space. Another one helped me source material. Together, they really helped out to get me started with teaching others how to drape. I didn't think that would happen with how this industry is, but they really welcomed me with open arms. Coming to Atlanta forced me to stretch the virtual side of my business and build an online community because I didn't know anyone. It truly was a clean slate.

Life for me at that point was surreal. I was transitioning from an 1,800-square foot house to a 3,000-square foot home. I had all this space, but I didn't hear the laughter from all my children. It was like a really emotional roller coaster. Still, I was just enjoying it. There were no gunshot sounds, police sirens, or thumping music blasting from car speakers. My biggest fear was the Atlanta traffic and accidents. Heck, I'd take that any day over the mean streets of Baltimore. It made me optimistic that if all this could happen this fast, there was so much more in store for me.

EXERCISE: ON TO BIGGER AND BETTER

1. What are your business goals?

___

___

___

2. Why did you choose that goal?

___

___

___

3. How will you know when you've achieved it?

___

___

___

4. What steps will you take to achieve it?

GOOD, BAD, AND UGLY

I want to elaborate more on how I became "The Draping Queen." Once I got my professional training and became certified with draping in Baltimore, I started to shift my business model. Again, I didn't go to school and trainings to drape events. My strategy was to go, learn the process, come back, and help other people that were frustrated like me.

After a while, I became the go-to person online. If they had a question about draping, they could come to me. I created a group strictly for draping and then it just blossomed into something more. They called me The Draping Queen because that became my primary focus once I decided to niche down.

Before the good started to happen, I did have some moments that tested my willpower. One of those was dealing with B-list celebrities. Now, on the surface, anyone would be psyched to work with someone that they've seen on TV. I still remember one of the first ones I did. Another designer had reached out and asked for my draping services.

Let me be clear about something before I go into this story. Celebrities are *not* my audience. I don't want to serve celebrities, and this situation is one of the many reasons why. Okay, back to the story. So, the designer explained to me that it was going to be a shower, and they told me what the person wanted. At this point in my journey, I was already talking to people that I wanted to talk to. I'd found my price, and that's the price I wanted to charge. I wasn't about to be haggled by nobody.

This particular planner was frustrated because their client was being plain ol' cheap. They said their client didn't have that amount in the budget and was trying to talk me down. I wasn't having it, so I pretty much ended the conversation right then and there.

Well, they ended up calling back and trying to piece together an offer that I would be happy with. You know how it is. "Well, what if you do *this*, but take *this* off, and then do *that*?" I remember sitting there thinking, *Oh, here we go.* Still, I had that little sliver of hope. You know that little voice that says, "If you just get this *one* celebrity event done to put on your page, it'll all be worth it." So, I told myself that I would take one for the team and just max out their budget the best way I could.

I went through with it, but the whole time I'm just kicking myself. I should have listened to my gut. Working with that person was one of the most trying events I've ever had. They had toxic energy on setup day and just seemed plain ol' ungrateful. Essentially, it was that sense of entitlement that really *really* turned me off.

The sad part is that I only experienced that negativity when I got celebrity requests. I've dealt with some frugal people before, but it got to be ridiculous. I would tell them that it's a $4,000 gig, and almost every single time they would try and haggle you down because they feel like their celebrity-ism deserved them a discount.

On top of that, the audience in itself was a struggle to work with. Think about it. My inventory is primarily fabric drapes. If I am hired for an event where there's knowingly going to be a lot of marijuana, that would damage my inventory. I know that I'm not going to risk my entire business just for the sake of one gig. So, I became really prone to saying no to celebrity events of that caliber. My attitude may change in the future, but as it stands today, it's a big no.

What I learned was the power of respecting yourself and your craft. We are all grown. I don't care how much money you have in your account; you're going to treat me with the same respect that I'm going to give you. Otherwise, all this stuff—including my draping supplies—will be up and be out.

To be blunt, my energy doesn't match well with people like that. I started from the ground and worked my way up. I didn't get any handouts. Therefore, I don't give them. If I'm providing a service, I'm selective about who I want to work with. I have left too many events early on in my business where I was underpaid, overworked, and irritated.

With that, I'm going to leave you with something that I heard not too long ago. We [people] take insurance for everything we care about. We take it out on our houses, cars, valuables, and even our lives. If we have insurance for all those things, then why not have some insurance for your energy and peace?

In other words, you want to protect your peace at all times. I *know* what kind of element I like to be in to just feel amazing and peaceful. If something comes along to disrupt that, then I'm just not going to do it. I will say a fast no before I say a slow yes.

EXERCISE: THE GOOD, BAD, & UGLY

1. Who is your target market?

____

____

____

2. Describe your ideal client?

____

____

____

3. What solution do you provide for them?

____

____

____

4. Who is NOT your ideal client?

___

___

___

5. Who do you desire to one day work with?

___

___

___

3-STEP FRAMEWORK

With everything that I've been through during my process, I was able to divide it up into a three-step framework. My framework is all about progression. It's one thing to know how to do something, but it's something else entirely to do it the *right* way and gain success from it. I wanted to grow my business for the long haul, so I focused on the following three areas of business that hinder most business owners: mastery, mindset, and marketing.

Before I could even *attempt* to get deep into this business, I had to master a few things. One of which was my skillset of mastering premium draping. I had to learn the actual skills to perfect my craft in a professional setting instead of just trying to wing it. Let's pause and talk about that for a second because this is important. Let's say you're a hairstylist. You've been doing hair in your kitchen for umpteen years, and now you've decided that you wanted to be a celebrity stylist. In order to do that, you're going to have to present yourself in a way that is appealing to celebrities, which is now your new target. You think that they're going to look at you if all you do is post photos of your clients from inside of your kitchen?

Unfortunately, they probably won't because it's not nearly as professional as someone who is in a salon providing a plush experience. In other words, you're not operating in a professional setting. You may be good at what you do, but if you can't translate those skills into a *professional* setting, it's going to be very difficult to scale yourself and your business the way that you want to.

One of the main goals I hear entrepreneurs wanting to achieve is "attract a higher paying client." If I am paying a premium price to have my hair done, I expect to have a premium experience. I don't expect to sit in your kitchen, hovering over a sink while people running in and out while I am getting my hairdo done.

Furthermore, in this stage, you want to be sure that your skillset is superb. I'm talking 5-star service and quality every single time that you work in your craft. To ensure that you're at your best, you have to be willing to invest in yourself and your business. Pay for the things that you *don't* know. During my journey, the only thing that was preventing me from achieving success early on was a lack of knowledge. If you truly desire to be at a certain level, the only thing stopping you from getting there is knowing how to do it.

Therefore, the quickest way to mastery is to enhance your skillset and then ultimately invest in what it is that you don't know. Find a mentor or coach who is successful at the thing you desire to achieve. Also, continuous learning is something that will always be key for long-term success. It's not a set it and forget it type of thing. You have to keep that same energy throughout your journey if you want to *stay* successful once you get there.

Let's be real about something. Every time you set out to reach a certain goal, you're going to want more. If you're ambitious like I am, you just can't help yourself. Realistically, once you get to that level you wanted to reach as your goal, you're going to continuously want to achieve *higher* goals if you're in the proper mindset. Remember, the only thing that's going to keep you from reaching those goals is the knowledge of knowing *how* to do so. So, you have to continuously educate yourself, research, and invest in your business to keep growing because anything that's not growing is pretty much dead.

You don't get into this journey of entrepreneurship just to be stagnant. You don't want to reach a certain plateau and that's it. You want to continuously grow and take it to the next level. To do that, you need to always be willing to invest and stop second-guessing whether it's necessary to do *this* training or *that* mastermind. Allow me to answer that question for you: it's a requirement. There's no way to get around it if you *really* want to grow. Knowledge without application is useless!

When I first started with this whole drapery game, I tried to watch DIYs and YouTube videos. I tried to ask people what to do, but everybody was tight-lipped. I didn't want to go to the big institutions at the time because I didn't want to pay all that money when I was still in the beginning stages. I wasn't willing to invest in myself. With that came a lot of frustration because I didn't know how to achieve this thing I wanted to achieve which was premium draping.

As a result, I was frustrated time after time getting lowball offers, until I finally made a decision to invest in myself with professional training. Once I did that, I was able to immediately start changing my services and attract a different kind of clientele.

Now, even though my business was set up for success, there was still something missing. I had learned and mastered my skillset, but I still didn't have confidence in myself. I had doubts about my self-worth, which had me scared to charge premium prices. Even though I knew how to design and attract *who* I wanted aesthetically, I didn't know how to position my business to be *ready* for the increase. So, I was still designing and not charging my worth.

Getting out of that mindset was challenging, but I knew it was necessary if I wanted to get that wealth. I started reading books and listening to all kinds of inspirational people, such as Eric Thomas and Mel Robbins. I would listen to these motivational speakers because every time I listened, I felt closer to understanding that I *deserved* more. When I finally felt like I was ready to charge more, I still needed to learn how to position my business or even host a consultation properly to *demand* more. I still was dealing with all that past childhood trauma, so I needed to invest in a coach to help me get my mind right for elevation. I had a couple of different coaches I went through before I found one who could really give me what I was looking for.

One of the coaches I had was good at helping me see the value that I provided. One of my exercises was to create an admiration album. Everyone was praising me and my work online. Not just from a drapery standpoint but as a person as well. People were always giving me positive feedback and telling me how good of a person I was.

At first, I said thank you and just shrugged it off. With this exercise, I was able to see all of these things together, and it did something to me. Internally, I *felt* different. I started realizing that yo, I am dope as f*ck! All of those can'ts in my head became cans. That self-doubt I was experiencing slowly started to disappear.

Another exercise I used to do was get challenged to go live. I didn't have to do it in front of my audience, but she wanted me to go live to myself, then record it. I did that, and she made me watch it and asked me, "What are you so scared of?" I started asking myself the same question when I saw the energy and charisma in that video. Why would I withhold this dopeness from other people? They *need* this. They need to see my personality.

From there, we would do test broadcasts. I would go live to my people for a smooth 10 minutes, and it was a dope 10 minutes. The more I went live authentically as Precious and not as a polished coach, the more love I got. I became comfortable in my own skin, and people responded positively to me loving being me. When you're walking in confidence, it increases the perceived value of how people see you. It took me probably a good six months to fully transition out of that negative, limiting mindset and realize that I deserved more. I was great at what I did, so I needed to be paid accordingly.

The third and final step is marketing. We all know that I thought marketing was all about the cute stuff. The websites, the logos, and the colors were all that mattered. I was spending so much money on "marketing," and I was confused on why I wasn't making the money I wanted to be making.

At the end of the day, my stuff was pretty but I didn't

know who I was talking to. I was just talking to anybody that was willing to book my services. My marketing wasn't clear until I started showing up and dealing with the mindset. Why? Because I wasn't able to connect deeper with my audience until I started to show my authentic self. I had to learn who loved *me,* what my solution was, and how to create messaging to speak directly to those people.

Marketing is the message that you are conveying to people. It's the perceived value of what they think you're worth. It has nothing to do with all of the cute stuff that I was working on when I first started my business. Once you get that message right, you can build a tribe and make money in your sleep. When you're clear on marketing with a strategy, you can identify with your audience and actually *have* the solution. Ain't no more haggling or even talking with Bargain Basement Betty no more. She's not even coming your way because she already knows she can't afford it.

On top of your messaging, you should have a good retention plan in place. It's one thing to land a *customer,* but there's a totally different thing when you land a *client*. Clients pay higher prices, and they are the ones that you enjoy working with. These people love everything you do, and you have the solution for exactly what they want. They don't haggle down your prices. Working with them is not a one-and-done situation. They will come back to you again and again, and they will start to develop a relationship with you. Most times, clients have more access than a customer would because clients are the ones who *you* pick.

Customers, on the other hand, are the ones who pick you. They want what you have. They may only come for your lower-tier products and services one time and then be done or shop often. Customers may not be your ideal client, but you usually can help them in some kind of way.

Once a *client* buys, you still have to nurture them like your babies. Even after the sale is over, you're still contacting them for other ways you can serve them deeper. You're still asking them do they need help. Essentially, you're still doing things to maintain the relationship.

Mastery, mindset, and marketing are how I was able to scale my business in an astronomical way. As tempting as it may be, you have to tackle all three. Trust me, you can and will see the difference.

EXERCISE: 3-STEP FRAMEWORK

1. Are you mentally prepared for the next comma club?

____

____

____

2. How satisfied are you with your current skill level?

____

____

____

3. How satisfied are you with your current marketing strategy?

____

____

____

4. If I held the solution to help you strengthen your business in these three areas, would you be interested?

____

____

____

5. What would you like to enhance or improve?

____

____

____

NOW

Now, I'm in a very soothing space in both my personal and my business life. I want to leave you with a few things that I hope you can take with you as you continue with your own journey. The first is to always maintain perspective. A lot of people just jump into business. They just keep going on and on with working, and they never stop to analyze what's really going on.

As a business owner, you need to constantly question and be aware of your business dealings. Monthly or even quarterly, analyze what's happening and what needs to change. If you don't take that time to pivot and take a look at your business holistically, then you risk it getting away from you. Before you know it, you may even have something that you don't even like anymore.

Take that time to step back and look at your business.

Determine if you need to add something or take something else away. Those little breaks are critical to your growth. I took that break after about 6 months in my business. I saw that things could be better, so I took that pivotal moment to step back and evaluate where it was and where it *could* be.

Now, I analyze the things I enjoy and things I don't, even in my business. I believe everything has the potential to be automated, outsourced, and delegated. It's up to me to determine what of those things I want to keep for myself and what I want to give to others. Doing so allows me to have a business I actually enjoy. The reason why is simple. When you're only doing things that you want to do, you're able to operate in your zone of genius.

A lot of people don't want to do that because they don't want to hire team members. They end up wearing 50 darn hats in their business and get frustrated because they're overworked. They forget how to find happiness in something that once used to have them excited.

I know what that's like. I used to do it too, even with relationships. I'm now in a successful partnership because I finally *know* what love means to me. I also know what it *looks* like, *feels* like, and even *smells* like for me. My business is successful because I know what I want to do. I know what my ideal lifestyle looks like. So, it's up to me to make it happen the way that I want it to.

Once my mindset changed in my business, it changed for me personally as well. I'm now focused more on the things that actually bring me joy. A lot of people say that, but I do it every day. If I don't like it, I ain't doing it. I don't care what it is. Think about it. How are you going to continue doing something long-term if you don't like what you're doing? Whether that be in a business or in a personal relationship, if you're not feeling it, don't do it.

Realistically, let's be clear. In business, there are some things that have to happen if you want your business to run efficiently. You can't just say you don't want to do accounting and boom, not have any bookkeeping aspect to your business. However, that doesn't mean that *you* have to be the one who does it.

When I first came to Atlanta, I didn't have a team. I had my own business, and I wanted to make it grow into something special. Now, that has since evolved to me having a team and 17 streams of income from this one business. I also have an overly fulfilling relationship that I've *never* experienced before. I have a life partner, and my heart feels like it is truly protected. I haven't felt that since before the death of my dad. He is the most consistent person I have ever experienced in life.

There's no question that my most recent successes are because of his support, love, and covering. He is more than just my partner; he is a spiritual being who loves deeply. He does nothing but supports any and *everything* that I do. Sometimes, it's scary how deeply connected we are.

I was on a personal development journey when he entered my life and my goal was to deeply explore and understand myself. My desire was to become a better version of Precious. I was in complete solitude for a little over a year. I wasn't looking to entertain any male counterparts, any dating, or hanging out since my divorce. I became a hermit. And here enters him in the buttermilk aisle...

The turning point in my development as an entrepreneur was when I started to trust again. Trusting the process and trusting *myself* was what allowed me to scale on the level that I'm at now as well as have a healthy relationship. I had to trust and believe that no matter what, I was not going to fail. Even if there are setbacks, failure could never happen. The whole thing is an experience, and I needed that experience to go along on this journey.

Anything I speak on and put into the universe will happen. Nothing is unrealistic, and the universe is responding favorably to my vibration right now. I've mentally and spiritually tapped into a space I've never, ever experienced. All of this came from just trusting. It's alright to share myself with the world. Everybody ain't going to *like* me, but it's a large number of people who *love* me, and I'm perfectly fine with that.

I *am* good enough.

You have to realize the same thing about yourself. Everything you need to be successful is within your reach. It may look a little raggedy in the beginning, but you just have to keep sowing the seeds. When they start sprouting, you're going to be on your knees every night saying thank you. It's going to be unbelievable. Then, when you *are* able to look back and see all that you've done, you will know that it was well worth it.

Oh, my God... it's *so* well worth it all.

All of those late nights crying and shedding tears will all be worth the fight. Don't think for a *second* that you're doing it for nothing. These past five years have been an absolute roller coaster. I've had some bad moments, but I've had even more life-changing ones. I'm in such a great space, connected to great people and there's much, much more to come.

I'm finally living life on my terms, and it feels absolutely amazing. I am not saying it isn't scary; however, I have survived worse. This is just the beginning!

EXERCISE: HOW I CAN HELP IMPROVE YOUR NOW

I teach creative professionals how to consistently attract higher-paying clients with my 3-step framework which allows them to make more money doing what they love.

I provide virtual and hands-on workshops on various skills to master your skillset so that you can become the highly sought out designer in your target market.

I provide virtual and hands-on coaching workshops teaching marketing strategies to help you discover your target audience and nail down your offer so you can get paid your worth by clients you enjoy working with.

To get started, simply download my 28-point business audit checklist so you can find the bottleneck in your business, which will allow me to properly resuscitate your business.

https://courses.precioussstevens.com/28-point

If you're ready to get actual help, simply book your strategy session to speak with me here:

www.precioussstevens.as.me

ACKNOWLEDGMENTS

I have to thank my awesome partner, Doc, for always believing in me and being my biggest cheerleader. From helping me decide cover pictures to book titles and tag lines. To being patient during those late night early morning proofreads and edits. I appreciate your support, love, faith, commitment, security, and love as well as simply helping me to trust, love, and feel to the depths that I never have before.

Thanks to my publisher, Bianca of BusyB Writing who made this process so simple and painless and created the dopest cover ever. You were able to take my story and convey it to the world in such an inspiring way. I thank you for all that you have done and look forward to us doing the sequel to *Anything's Poshable!*

I thank my bestie Yo-Yo for being just that, my bestie. You have always been my ride or die and have always cheered me on even when my faith wasn't as great. You had visions of me doing big things and would get frustrated when I wanted to play small and safe. From you, I have learned the true meaning of a sisterly bond and grew the desire to want to be a better person. I thank you and I am so excited to see what we do next. It's been a heck of a ride.

Although this book covers a lot of pain I faced early on in my life, my experience would not have been as valuable to inspire others if it had not been for my parents who provided me with the necessary tools to navigate through life's journey. Thanks to the late Quinton Stevens who instilled in me that "Anything's Poshable" along with my Mom, Beverly Johnson, who has helped me to understand how "Staying Poshitive" can easily shift all negative things and who has truly taught me the true meaning of forgiveness.

I thank my three children Jaheim, Kaden, and Kayla, who I can only hope one day fully understand the dramatic changes I have made. I can only hope that one day you fully understand that your purpose is bigger than you and you act on it immediately without blinking an eye. The changes I make today are for all of you to have a better tomorrow. My legacy will live on long after I am gone, and I owe it to you guys. I would not have had a desire to do better if you guys weren't mine. Just always remember, life is what you make it because "Anything's Poshable," and there's always light at the end of the tunnel. You'll get to it quicker by "Staying Poshitive."

I say thanks to my baby, the late Khloe. You have been with me through it all. You were my baby. I never understood how people were so attached to their pups, but you sure put it on me. I miss you, and I know you'd be right here the entire time sitting in my lap. Rule well in puppy heaven, as I know you are.

ABOUT THE AUTHOR

Have you ever felt that you were on this earth for something great but just haven't found what it was yet?

Precious Stevens wasn't always the savvy entrepreneur she is today. Precious is driven by the belief that there is always light at the end of the tunnel. This faith has allowed her to launch Posh Designs, LLC, The Posh Academy, as well as her newest venture, Grand Poshture Boutique.

Precious is a Baltimore, Maryland native. She always had a knack for creative innovations and providing a "POSH" flavor to everything she touched. Precious got a strong sense of urgency to launch her event business in 2016 after growing tired of her corporate gig that had no upward mobility. As she saw elegant drapery designed by various professionals, she fell in love and found her niche.

In 2020, the Covid-19 Pandemic hit, forcing The Posh Academy to postpone its 24-city tour for the remainder of the year. Upon relaunching the tour in 2021, her drive was stronger than ever, thus expanding into The Posh Network. Her passion for creativity makes her an innovator of ideas, her high energy and electric personality will invite you in and make you feel right at home. Precious is a solution-driven expert and her many years of experience will put you at ease when working with her.

Precious has jumped in the event space and hit the ground running, paving a way for many up-and-coming designers to learn premium draping. Her trailblazing efforts will continue to share her message of integrity, purpose, and faith, showing creatives that they have the power to do what they love AND achieve greatness doing it.

So, if you are tired of being creative and broke, you have picked up the right book. This guide is the first step in the right direction to growing your business.

Precious believes designers deserve more money and she helps them get it.

You can easily pair the workings in this book with Precious's free 28-point business audit at

https://courses.preciousstevens.com/28-point.

Get access to your download immediately!

Made in the USA
Columbia, SC
09 July 2022